Janthology

Elcin Nur

*To future Elch so she can either preen,
or cringe*

ACKNOWLEDGEMENT

To everyone that convinced me this was a great idea - I don't know why I believed you, but I'm glad I did.

PREFACE

I never once thought I'd publish a book of poetry
- it's the kind of wanky thing I'd talk about
without ever having any intentions toward it.
But when I accepted the challenge to try, it took
me on such a journey through old journals,
scrawled letters, sad memories and intense self
reflection, that I'm actually a little annoyed with
myself that I didn't do it earlier.

Despite my glibness, words really are my love
language. So if you're reading this, I want to say
a heartfelt thank you. Really. Every poem on the
next few pages was written in January 2023. I
hope you like them.

Kaiki

1

After the events of the day
we'd sluice the salt off our skin
and sit on the swings and talk, just you and I

The sun would set over the moody horizon
we'd still be spilling poison
about everyone we knew, just you and I

On the day we found that little boat
we'd thought about how to make it float
without experience, yes you and I

But grounded on the shore in sludge
we'd found the oars refused to budge, even for you and I

Night on the rooftop

2

It was your walk that got me
the lightness of your walk when you hunched your shoulders
the ambling lolling limbs
the way your feet never seemed to touch the ground

It was your smile that got me
The lightness of your smile when it broke over your face
the shattering beams flattering
the way your cheeks would stretch and dimple all around

It was your arms that got me
The lightness of your arms as they swung with your mood
the tapering and paper-white skin
the way you'd hold them open, like I was waiting to be found

Floods

3

When I think of wet things I think
of tranquil squelching underfoot or
trickles and ripples like brooks in woods
not the crippling floods I'd feel
when you were close by

When I think of wet things I think
of gently undulating waves
Soft seasprays and mizzle, misty drizzle
not the bitter floods I'd spill
when you made me cry

When I think of you I think
of turbulent insurgencies
When I think of you I think
of hot rivers bursting like emergencies

When I think of you I think of floods
still waiting to dry

Time travel

4

We don't face the future, we walk backwards into it
Blind men steeped in memories
Gingerly, with splayed out fingers
step by step to avoid injury

We don't turn from the past, we stay forwards facing it
Mankind stares into mirrors
Unthinking, shuffles away
day by day to watch their memories shrinking

Trip of a lifetime

5

The brightest images
are the ones we remember
Like that night in November when I asked you to step forward
into your hoarded memories
And find them with me

And you took me by the hand
And led me into your quiet scene
Where we were both 18, and meeting each other
in a place I'd never been

I'd give anything to be there once more with you
cross legged on the floor we
Close our eyes
and find we'd met before

Party Pals (an ode to Elf Bars)

You smell so sweet
And taste so good
You make nights out more easy
But every time I breathe you in
I'm out of breath and wheezy

Branches

You be the tree, and I'll be the snake
I'll slither up your trunk and take
full advantage of your branches
and let myself unfurl

Seeking your fruits, in a manner of speaking
Sinking my teeth til your boughs are leaking
those little pips and juicy drips
that glisten and impearl

Your crown of leaves, I'll sit in your green
Sneakily so I can't be seen
No spying eyes spot my disguise
I'm gone without a trace

And when winter strips us of our luck
I'll slide down and rejoin the muck
Of mulchy brown and frosty ground
And coil up at your base

Because I've been the snake and you've been the tree
I'll never wander far you see
And spring will come round once again
And with it bring your blossoms then
they'll shower down on me

Ditty for a dilettante

8

Sometimes I'm afraid to ask after the person behind your mask
It's such a task to learn a lesson
About people who don't want to be seen

Sometimes your changeability is your only source of constancy
Frivolity is such a phoney disguise
For who you are and you who've been

Sometimes you're like a ghost at a party that has lost its host
But I'm engrossed in your ability
To wipe your history clean

Sometimes your lines start shaking and your words get obfuscating
Then your fear's pulsating I can feel
The need to intervene

Sometimes your imagination is nothing but a thirst for validation
The medication all along was
Your face behind the screen

Another round

Let's not talk of intimacy, it's too notional
And I'm prone to getting emotional
When we discuss legitimacy

Let's not talk of heart, it's too conceptual
And I'm really no intellectual
When there's nothing to impart

Let's not talk of truth, it's too variable
And we're neither of us that marriable
When we've downed a drink or two
I don't care what this is
When we can practice kisses to see the evening through

Triangles

A triangle is a shape of hidden tangles
With three straight lines and three straight angles
Or if you view it another way
A triangle is a three act play
Act 1 is the side of exposition
Act 2 is the side of nuclear fission
Act 3 is a long side, it has a reprise
(This triangle is an isosceles)
But it'll sit quite stable, a pointer of pride
Until you try to remove a side
Then amidst a sequence of grand mishaps
Witness the whole shape collapse

Sugar cube

"I fell in love"
Sounds like defeat
And I don't understand it
"I fell in love"
Did you trip over your feet?
Had some other person planned it?
"I fell in love"
No, I disagree
Love wasn't a trap or a threat
If you were the sugar cube, then love was the tea
That gradually mushed you with wet
"I fell in love"
No, love rose in you
Like a sunrise that gently evolved
And stained your white crystals maroon in their hue
until you eventually dissolved

Play Doh

Sometimes I squeeze myself together
unmalleable and turgid
unable to merge with me or gather
myself intact
Like bits of dried out Play-Doh
Roll me into a ball
Colourful and cracked

Driver's seat

I need a cushion, darling please
I need a cushion to feel at ease
I need a cushion, something to sit on
I can't see over the wheel

I need a cushion, I'm veering and sliding
I need a cushion, I'm scared of colliding
Make a decision, I'm getting a vision
Of smoke and mangled steel

I need a cushion for the driver's seat
Because in my act of self-deceit
I sold the line, that I was fine
But my neck is starting to ache

And I have been as good as gold
Done everything that I was told
Smiling and sweet, in the driver's seat
With no intent to brake

But now I can't see the lanes or lines
Now I can't read the bloody signs
I"m going to stray, I'm losing my way
I needed a cushion from the start

Yes I need a cushion imminently
Your apathy is blinding me
I'm not overreaching, I'm only beseeching
A little support, I'm a little too short
Don't want you to fight back, I just want my sight back
I need a cushion, please I'm begging
Just do your fucking part

Turkish fortune teller

14

It's just a coffee cup cooling upside down
with chic little lipstick prints on its rim
I'm glad she saw the state I was in
And offered to tell her own

Dad's teaspoon

15

Who knew metal on skin could be so gentle, dad?
The silky skim of steel
that scooped the salty rain from each cheek
one sad day
Who knew you could feel two things at once, dad?
The tender consoling grief
that collected the droplets you called precious
The indignance that flung them away

Selfishness

You couldn't let me go at once
So you hacked me into pieces
And gradually tossed them away
I guess it was easier
At least for you that way
And look, I get it
But let me know
When you are done
If that's okay

How to forgive

Last night I wore your clothing
    (I bought a too-big shirt from TK Maxx)
And I walked around in your shoes
    (I stole a pair of my dad's boots)
And I channelled my inner loathing
    (I ate a kilo of unhealthy snacks)
And I masked a bit with booze
    (I drank a wanky beer you'd choose)
And I raised my pen, wrote "I was wrong"
    (I scrawled "I was an inconsiderate prick")
And all the reasons why
    ("Because I forced you to carry my grief")
And apologised that it took so long
    ("I'm a cowardly emotionally illiterate dick")
To give humility a try
    ("A hubristic patience thief")
Then I ripped the page at the perforation
    ("And it's almost like I'm too uptight")
Scrunched it up with mad frustration
    ("To grow some balls and do what's right")
Took it out and built a pyre
    ("But don't think I want you to worry")
And set the fucking thing on fire
    ("I know you know, I'm truly sorry")

Play Doh 2 (The Symposium)

18

Eh, maybe Aristophanes had a point
Sometimes I feel so disjointed
Like one half of me can't merge with the other
Like my two halves can't come together
So maybe if you put my pieces in a seat
and held them in the heat of your hand
it would make me feel better

Squeeze me until I beg for release
Maybe I'll melt and come out in one piece

Portakal

19

I once had a dream
about a bowl of oranges on a table
The only splash of colour in the room
Little orbs of brightness
carrying the promise of liquid sunshine
But as I drew closer
I saw the skins were mottled
and the flies sat on their flesh and laid their eggs within the
grooves
So I stepped myself away
And I willed myself to wake